In Spiritus Theos

A Collection of Divinely Inspired and Channelled Poetry

BRETT NELSON

BALBOA PRESS
A DIVISION OF HAY HOUSE

Copyright © 2016 Brett Nelson.

All rights reserved. No part of this book may be used or reproduced by any means, graphic, electronic, or mechanical, including photocopying, recording, taping or by any information storage retrieval system without the written permission of the author except in the case of brief quotations embodied in critical articles and reviews.

Balboa Press books may be ordered through booksellers or by contacting:

Balboa Press
A Division of Hay House
1663 Liberty Drive
Bloomington, IN 47403
www.balboapress.com
1 (877) 407-4847

Because of the dynamic nature of the Internet, any web addresses or links contained in this book may have changed since publication and may no longer be valid. The views expressed in this work are solely those of the author and do not necessarily reflect the views of the publisher, and the publisher hereby disclaims any responsibility for them.

The author of this book does not dispense medical advice or prescribe the use of any technique as a form of treatment for physical, emotional, or medical problems without the advice of a physician, either directly or indirectly. The intent of the author is only to offer information of a general nature to help you in your quest for emotional and spiritual well-being. In the event you use any of the information in this book for yourself, which is your constitutional right, the author and the publisher assume no responsibility for your actions.

Any people depicted in stock imagery provided by Thinkstock are models, and such images are being used for illustrative purposes only.
Certain stock imagery © Thinkstock.

Print information available on the last page.

ISBN: 978-1-5043-5455-4 (sc)
ISBN: 978-1-5043-5456-1 (e)

Balboa Press rev. date: 04/15/2016

For
Farah, Sofia and Duke
Who taught me unconditional love

Contents

Introduction and Author's Notes ix
Poems for those Who have Gone Ahead 1
Haiku Season 11
Poems of the Night 17
Poems of the I Am 29
In the Wake of the Wake RUMInations on a Voyage 39
Poems of Healing 45

Introduction and Author's Notes

This book is the end of the first stage of a journey that began a little more than three years ago. It started at the worst time in my life. I went through a period of darkness, depression, imprisonment and healing which culminated in what you see here. This is an expression of my healing and acceptance of the beauty and grandeur of life.

Had I been paying attention, this process would have been much shorter and less painful, but some of us need to go through the darkness to begin to glimpse the light. For all that it took, I am grateful and look forward to whatever should be awaiting me on the next stages of my journey.

Like many people, I was highly dubious of claims of 'channelling' spirits and entities from other times and dimensions. Although I have always been a spiritual questor, I felt that these claims bordered on the ridiculous, and I treated any accounts of this nature with extreme scepticism.

It was not until the end of an incredible journey in the Mediterranean with Dr Wayne Dyer (See section 5, In the Wake of the Wake) when I was literally overtaken with the creative spirit, that I realized that such things were indeed possible. With my mind opened by the wonder of my journey, and the beauty of the Italian countryside, I was overwhelmed with the compulsion to write and the words began to flow forth. Each time that I thought that I was done, an inner voice compelled me to put pen to paper and start again.

So prolific was the voice that day, that in the 3 hours it took to travel from the port of Civitavecchia, to the airport in Rome and fly halfway to Frankfurt I had penned the 10 poems you find in section 5. I do not say that I wrote them, because upon looking at them after having written them, I did not recognize the words as my own or as having come from me. As I read them, it was as if I was reading someone else's work for the first time.

So it has continued since that day. Quite often I am filled with the need to write poems, and other works. When I allow myself to be open to this process, I need only grab my pad and pen and sit quietly while the muse works through me. I do not feel the passage of time, nor any emotion save that of divine inspiration.

Upon finishing, I am filled with a sense of peace, joy and a belonging to something that is so very much greater than myself. Some of my favourite works in this book have taken no longer than ten minutes, mainly because I am a slow writer. As I have become somewhat acquainted with this creative spirit, I have begun to see how our relationship works and can comfortably feel some small sense of ownership in the process.

I write the poems down exactly as they come to me. I make no grammatical, punctuation or structural changes. When I first attempted to edit the poems I was overcome with a strong sense that it was not my place to do so. As such, the poems you see here are in the same exact form as they were dictated to me, with no alterations whatsoever. This is also why some have titles and some don't. If the spirit does not supply one I do not ask.

Not all of the poems here are channelled. Some I wrote the old fashioned way of being inspired and taking several hours to come up with an acceptable piece. Even so, I feel that the ultimate authority was still the spirit that inspired me. In that regard I realize that it is all one; that all the poems and all the creative inspiration comes from the one same place. I have been blessed enough to have been used by it.

Unfortunately, my ego still gets in the way. Several times over the last few years, the spirit has come to me at times that I felt were inconvenient.

Some times I have been working and felt that it was too difficult to stop work to write. Other times I have been busy with trivial things, or have been in situations that I felt might make stopping to write a poem to be embarrassing. Often I have tried to store the inspiration on the back burner for use at a more convenient time, only to have it fade away with the poetic idea never coming again. Life has always been and continues to be a never ending lesson in what is truly important.

I truly hope that you enjoy this collection of poems as much as I have enjoyed the process of bringing them to you. I humbly hope that they bring to you some semblance of the peace, joy, awe and wonder that they inspired in me.

May God bless you, as I feel he has blessed me. May you feel the light and the warmth of his love, and may you find your own spirit and create the beauty you were intended for.

Love,
Brett Nelson

POEMS FOR THOSE WHO HAVE GONE AHEAD

Often times there are so many things we need, want or desire to say to someone in our lives, but lack the courage or opportunity to do so. Sometimes the basis of a relationship does not allow sentiment to find its way into the open. We all have things to say that are not easy, nor sometimes even possible to share with people who have touched our lives in some way. I know myself that many of the things I wished I'd said to my parents weren't even in my experience to do so while they were alive.

These few poems are my attempt to convey the feelings that I was never able to while these relationships were accessible to me. As do most poems of this nature they attempt to close the book, even the score, settle the debt, give thanks, pay homage and give credence that the lessons were learned though maybe not right away.

"Thoughts on A Normandy Beach" is very special to me. It brought my relationship with my father to completion with an understanding that I did not have when the events that inspired it occurred. This poem is also the subject of the cover photo of this book. It is a photo I took of my father (a D-Day veteran) on a Normandy beach a few months before he died.

Two of the poems in this section are for my mentor Dr Wayne Dyer. I feel that without his influence I would never have believed in myself enough to put these efforts together for publication. When I heard of his passing I realized that it was time to put my work out there. The poems about him are my way of saying thank you to the teacher who woke me and helped me find my music.

I'm not really sure what I want people to make of, or do with these poems. More than anything I think this section allows me to share what the spirit had to share with me regarding death and any unexpressed intentions left in its wake. Perhaps by reading these poems, some of you will be inspired to pay homage in your own way and close some of the books that have been left open by those in your life who have passed. Perhaps they will convey a feeling of closure to you. In any event, they are here for your perusal.

In Spiritus Theos

*

Always with me, your voices carry
Always with me, your gentle touch
Ever with me, your love and caring
Never far from me the joy of you

Years ago I mourned your leaving
Not knowing then what is true
You never left, how could you?
There is only here

With me always I hear and feel you
In the morning with my first thoughts
During the day in my remembrances,
In the evening you guide my prayers
At night you star in my dreams

I close my eyes to see you
Open my ears to hear
You are in me always
Never away, ever near
Always with me

*

Brett Nelson

Thoughts on a Normandy Beach

You walked away from me that day
And never really returned
And so the circle closed
That day so long ago
That grey day
The grey of the clouds
That matched the sand
The grey of the cold cold sea
That echoed the greyed and ancient
Memories of that same beach
In a very different time
What did you see that day?
What ghosts did you meet,
What nightmares confronted you?
Should I know or should I rest
Assured that you are reconciled
To a past not entirely of your own making
Are you free of the terrors that
Shaped both our lives
Of a past that never faded
No matter how much it was
Drowned or buried
Did you find the peace that
Eluded you all our time together
On that faraway beach in another land
In another world
In another time

*

For Wayne

O Blessed soul
You came to teach
You came to educate, to open minds
To enlighten
You came to bless
To celebrate, to savour.

O Blessed soul
You came to share
To enable joy
To foster understanding and love
You came to forgive
To spread peace
To help us find ourselves.

O blessed soul
You came to lessen
The fears and woes
Explore consciousness
Help us discover silence
And revel in the quiet knowing of God.

But you were never this
This striving, straining
Competition, driving
Rushing helter skelter
You were never this
Climbing, struggling
Unfulfilled anxiousness
That so permeates this world

Brett Nelson

So how could you stay
It wearies the best and brightest
And you were more than that
Before it bent and withered you
Corrupted and beat you down
You went.

O blessed soul
Your lessons stay with me
Your guidance my light
All that you brought
Is forever kept sacred
Remembered and honoured
My armour against despair
My music against the din and clamour
The silence of my prayer
The quiet of my soul
'Tis all your gift

*

To My Mentor

Unending undying love
You taught me
All that I AM you are
You lifted veils from my eyes
And weight from my heart
Now you sit beside me
Unseen by my common conscious
Yet known and felt by my being
Free of the need for words
Unfettered and unchained
Delivered of your earthly limits
I mourn only for myself
That you are not available to my needs.
In truth you are now perfect
You are where I would be
Where I must be anon
As the seed must become the sprout
And the sprout become the flower
You are blossomed
Full realized in potential and beauty
Shining and radiant
Truly one with all
Undying life you once taught me
Life is infinite, joy unlimited
Now you are that and more
And speak to me in dreams

Brett Nelson

Little Man My Hero

Little man you saved me
You came to me
At the worst of times
A gift from on high
To change my world
A deliverance of immense proportion
In the smallest of packages.

Little man you changed me
And with that my life
With a spirit far too large
For such a tiny body
An aura far too bright
To shine on just one person
You spread your magic far and wide

Little man you inspired me
And the many lives you touched
Your beautiful soul
Your tangible, undeniable love
Felt by all who knew you
A reminder that the greatest gifts of heaven
Come in forms unexpected
And with value unimagined
And no one knows how long they are here
But it's never long enough

Little man I miss you
Little man I love you
Little man my hero

*

*

Today is the day for tears
For he is gone
Our son and brother
Friend teacher and lover
He is gone from us
And we must mourn
Today is the day to cry
To weep to lament
A day for the wringing of hands
The tearing of clothes
Of condolences suffering and woe
But only today
For tomorrow begins anew
And life carries on, heedless
The light brings warmth and healing
Tomorrow we are grateful
For what he gave us
And what he took
We thank creation
For the time we spent
In his presence and his light
And we grow well knowing
That every moment was a gift
And his was given wisely and well
As tomorrow becomes today
And passes by as all must do
We rejoice from then on
That he has returned from whence he came
At one with time
That even by his passing
We are made more whole
For now we have one more angel
One more particle of God
Looking directly upon us
To bring us home

Brett Nelson

*

My friend when will we meet
Will you sing to me again
Will you smile that smile
That seemed only mine
Will you laugh the laugh
That I thought only I could bring
So much of you that did not die
I see alive in others
I never knew before
And the joy becomes in knowing them
But still I miss that smile
That laugh, the knowing behind the eyes
That gentle something I will not see
Until we meet again my friend

*

Haiku Season

I have always admired the precision of Haikus. In each one you find seventeen perfectly chosen and arranged syllables, symbolizing a complete train of thought perfectly captured in a brief statement. A haiku is the essence of succinct. Yet if properly done each three line unit can inspire volumes of speculation, opinion and dialogue as to the nature of its meaning. In this lies the true beauty of the art form.

Haikus are so much deeper than their brief and compact form would suggest. Their meanings are complex and always require more scrutiny than just one reading will allow. The choosing of the right word in the right place to convey the right sentiment is the one thing that has always drawn me to see haikus as a poetry of immense wisdom. As for the title of this section, I always thought that the word Haiku sounded like some sort of weather event that might happen in the spring and bring about the end of cold weather or something like that.

So I present to you my attempts at this noble literary form. I do not claim to have achieved, let alone mastered, the intricacies and/or complexities of this unique form of expression. I only share as the spirit shared with me, and hope that you find enjoyment in our efforts.

Brett Nelson

*

I Am Blest with fortune
I AM loved because I love
God smiles upon me

*

Good morning my God
In all things do I see you
You are my whole world

*

To know I AM love
Is to know I create life
And am one with God

*

Death does not exist
There is no heaven or hell
Only life and love

*

Life is beautiful
When you are one with spirit
And naught else matters

*

In Spiritus Theos

*

A special something
Without which I am nothing
The divine within

*

Disavow the flesh
Seek union with the spirit
In this lies your truth

*

You are not the one
To anguish over life's ills
You have faith in God

*

Love's divine music
A chorus of quietude
Sings God's symphony

*

The veil is lifted
Death stands before you no more
Life is infinite

*

Brett Nelson

*

I allow God's Love
To dissipate my ego
And make me holy

*

Salty tears of joy
From the beauty around me
My union with God

*

In reality
Forgiveness does not exist
True love has no need

*

My self dwells in love
Who I AM resides in joy
Life, a prayer of thanks

*

Fear of surrender
Is all that separates us
From living in God

*

*

Inspiration lies
Beneath the cloudy cover
Of indifference

*

Eight kilometres
A good long run each morning
Free enlightenment

*

Illusions abound
But the voice of God is true
Calling us each day

*

Mirror reflection
Staring back at me is God
Behind my own eyes

*

A little on the irreverent side
Thanks God, by the way
You do some pretty good work
Big guy, ya know that?

*

*

Ashes to ashes
That which we were we become
And life continues

*

Song of evening
No words are necessary
Love is melody

*

Mists on the river
Morning's mysteries abound
Consciousness beckons

*

Enlightenment means
Knowing time does not exist
We still sit and wait

*

I see you there God
Being behind my own eyes
Where else would I be?

*

POEMS OF THE NIGHT

To me the night has always held a special significance. I find that there is a very magical beauty in the transformation from light to dark and back again. I have never truly been one to be afraid of the dark. As a small child, although I was certain that many questionable entities were lurking when the lights were turned off, I was always quite sure that I was protected as long as I said my prayers and covered up properly.

I grew up in a small town, with a father who loved the outdoors and insisted on sharing that love with me. As such, my childhood was filled with open skies and starry nights. I don't know whether I was particularly precocious in that way, or it was the nature of my culture, but even as a young boy I felt the energy and magic and even the spirits that came alive at after dark.

I grew up believing in banshees, woods people, fairies and the like but never felt threatened by them, only curious as to what it all meant and how it all came together. The night time world for me was a distinctly different world from that of the day. Filled with its own rules and definitions, the night world filled me with a sense of wonder equally as large as that of the day but almost diametrically opposed in its difference.

As a searcher for spiritual truth in my adult years, I came to believe in the power of dreams. A lot of this belief came from my heritage, as dreams are considered extremely powerful messages in aboriginal culture. I grew up as a dreamer and believer in the specialness of dreams, and have always had a yearning to understand their nature and their meaning.

One fascinating aspect (I find) that is common to both dreams and night, is that man cannot consciously control either without changing their nature so much as to make them something else entirely. They have mystery, consciousness and a life of their own quite separate from us and just a little unnerving. Perhaps this is why humans spend so much energy attempting to explain and eradicate both night and dreams in order to make them more understandable or less threatening, respectively.

In any event, night and dreams are filled with their own poetry, and are the inspiration for many of mine. I hope that you enjoy these.

*

O little man who holds me
It's time to close your eyes
Time to slumber, time to dream
To release me from your clutches
Do let me free. Home I would be
Unleashed and unfettered
In my element, my sea.
You've had your day
The night is mine
To dance and frolic
With my own kind
I would walk a million miles
To my home amidst the stars
And stranger lands than you would know
Are where I find my heaven
When you die each night
I come alive, and become what I AM destined
No limits can you place on me now
Though never do I leave you lonely
For all I AM is just for you
Though you refuse to see
And when you wake
With crusty eyes
Bewildered and bemused
Remembering little if any of my doings
I shall sit where you place me
Awaiting the night and the chance to be
As I was meant
When you close your eyes and allow

*

Brett Nelson

*

A shrouded moon hangs
In the summer night sky
Backlighting clouds for a portrait
By a sublime artist
A clouded moon meanders
Across an August night sky
With a carefree glint in her eye
Knowing her way
A well danced moon settles herself
In the valley of a lightened sky
All on a warm summer morning
Her admirers and lunatics all
Fully sated

*

Twilight
The raspberry glow of sunset
Gives way and fades to the dusky hue
Of twilight
Stillness falls upon the vale
And all who dwell in light
Surrender to a darker beauty
And close their eyes
To dream tomorrow's destiny
The robins and the deer
The wrens and the voles
Like their brother the sun
Lay down their heads for
God filled slumber
While above and around them
The children of the moon
Make ready to dance
Their nightly waltz
In their mother's silvered harmony

*

In Spiritus Theos

*

Quietly, Softly, Tenderly
The many hued beauty transforms the landscape
What were once sharply defined contrasts
Become duskily vague outlines
And the light, like a nomadic caravan
Moves merrily ever onward
Westerly, westerly
In search of new lands to ignite
Thus eventide descends
And sits gently on the trees and mountains
Sings it's delicate lullaby and keeps watch
As the valley sleeps and dreams of a new
Morning and the return of the luminous caravan

*

From this dream I reach
Through layers of cloud
Past countless stars
To the edge of infinity itself
To touch the face of God
To take my place in light
And shine in glory undiminished
Both humbled and glorified am I
To reach my destiny, my ultimate truth
And be what has always been
Yet still the dream persists
And the world goes on before me
As before changing, challenging
Seemingly unending, uninterested
and unfulfilled
With but one difference
For now I know
It is just a dream

*

Brett Nelson

*

Fear not the dark
Fear not the night
Fear not the winter
They hold no power
For all are merely passings
Mere vistas at roadside
Not worthy of a stop
Nor more than a glance
And each but a marker pointing way
To a new spring
A new morning
A new light
Such as thine eyes have never seen

Rejoice
For the new day is stronger than the night
The spring more inevitable
And the light unstoppable
Unbowed by any dark
Endless, Eternal and transcendent
Awaiting all travellers
The endpoint of all journeys
A universal beginning

*

*

I Would Sleep

I would sleep
For I am weary
And the day is long
I would rest my head
And trust to God and angels
The flights of my soul
In its' brief respite
From the toils of the earth

Oh I would sleep
For the world of men is trying
It harries and harasses
It cajoles and coerces
And silence and joy
Are scarce commodities
In a world that little values peace

Brett Nelson

Yea I would sleep
For the night is soft and warm
It beckons with dreams
And I would lay my head
On the soft earth
And be seduced
By dark slumber's promise
Of gentle rest

Yes I would sleep
And wake another day
To sunshine light and joyful
To peace eternal
In fragrant fields
And melodies sweet
I would toil no longer
But rest with God and angels
In the quietude of love

*

With Apologies to Dylan Thomas

Do not rage
The light will not die
Tho the candle may flicker
The flame lives on abundantly
Why resist when all
Is as must be
The candle is nothing
The light is all
The wicks to carry it
Are many, and when they tire
They do not end
But are transformed
To light themselves
As all must be

Do not rage
With every step go gently
The path beneath is cushioned
Festooned with blossom
Garlanded with blessing
None need fear the night
Neither good nor evil, only night

Do go. Go gently
Through lace and gossamer
Black and fine
A dark and misty veil
That yields to eternity
Once breached
Do not rage
All is as all must be

*

Brett Nelson

*

Silhouettes and shadows
The currency of night
Stealth and cunning are your champions
You silence the day
And envelop your domain
In a shroud of mystery and secret
But I do not fear
I see right through you
You are the alter
The other stripe
The camouflage through which the sun
Might hide his face and rest awhile
Without you he is little
Without you there is naught to compare
Nor would he shine so brightly in man's eye

In Spiritus Theos

Shadows and silhouettes
The current and sea of night
Flowing quietly through your air
You silence the light
Though you may rage and storm
Be fogged and clouded
At times, I see
Through you that patience
And thereby wisdom
Are not born
From the heat and tumult of the day
But in the peace and stillness of your hours
In a world made calm and still
With quiet expectation
And calm anticipation of the day
Which naturally follows
And again gives way to you
I do not fear
You are as much a home to me
As is your loud and boisterous brother
You are my respite from the day

*

POEMS OF THE I AM

P robably the most important book that helped keep me on the spiritual path during my incarceration was Dr. Wayne Dyer's "Wishes Fulfilled". As any who have read it know, the main theme of the book is I AM (the name of God as revealed to Moses and the identity of each and every human's highest self). The comfort, strength and inspiration I received from reading this book is inestimable.

Throughout that time, I AM was my constant mantra. When I awoke, it was the first thought on my mind and the first words from my lips. All through the day I reminded myself of what my life could be, by repeating "I AM" with my deepest God inspired desires. At night it gave me the comfort and absolute knowing that allowed me peaceful, healing sleep.

The beauty of I AM is that it truly is infinite. The divine and wonderful thoughts and ideas that you can say after these two words are endless, and with proper use of imagination or inspiration, poetic. Just sitting and allowing my consciousness to consider all the things that I AM is enough for me to brighten the darkest days or lift the heaviest burdens from my shoulders. I have often been inspired to write poems that reflect the spirit of the I AM as it makes itself known to me. The works you see in this section are the results of that inspiration.

Once again, these poems are transcribed here exactly as they came to me, and I claim poetic and artistic license for any questionable grammar. You will notice as in all of my work, there are no titles except where one was supplied by the Spirit.

*

Just as the pen is but a means to expression
So I AM nothing more than an implement
To Spirit's desire to be heard
My thoughts are ink putting form
To joy and wonder
The inspiration flows from beyond
Imagining
Through me and pen alike
To become symbols on a page
Should any of it prove worthy or divine
I rest assured, it is not I
Who creates a thing
I, like the pen, am merely a link in the chain
A small part in an infinite process
But unlike the pen, I AM
Possibly, just possibly, more
Grateful for the opportunity to be so

*

Divine All
I AM the writer of all poems
I AM the singer of all songs
I AM the player, the instrument
The muse and the pen
I AM the sculptor, the potter
The painter, the piece
I AM the director of the myriad plays
I AM the inspiration and the audience
I AM the author of this
And every world
I AM creation
I AM the All in All

*

*

I AM inspired by the slightest touch from God
My grandest ideas are but the faintest of creation's whispers
Like the fluff of a dandelion I AM carried along on the fairest breeze
Joyfully wafted, huffed hither and yon
In a pattern not of my own design
Trusting in the guidance and wisdom
Of that which created me
Knowing that the endpoint of my journey
Is and will be sweeter than
All my imaginings
For I AM love transcendent

*

Who I AM is infinite
Who I AM is endless
Who I AM has never slept
Has seen every sunrise
And counted every star
Who I AM has cried every tear
And falls with every snowflake
Who I AM is in every tumbling leaf
And every drop of rain
I AM every ray of sunshine that ever shone
Before all that was, is and ever shall be
I AM

*

Brett Nelson

*

Wrapped in the arms of God
I AM as a child in mother's embrace
Where all is safe and warm
And all is right and good
Invincible and protected
I AM free to imagine
All that could possibly be
All that is potentially me

Wrapped in the arms of God
I AM where I belong
Where I have always been
Infinitely alive, free of all
That could harm me
Free of a world that never existed
Immortal and infinite

*

I AM as I AM
With every breath
I AM creating
With every blink of an eyelid
Am I born again
With every tear of joy shed
That lightens my soul
I AM come
To the beauty so real
To the existence too exquisite
For this humanity to hold.

What I AM is all this
And so much more
I AM of an eternity unknown
I AM far more than this
I AM beyond words
I AM rapture

*

In Spiritus Theos

*

I AM cleansed
I AM bathed in the waters of love and peace
I AM washed in the spring of forgiveness.
I AM baptized in the font of eternal blessings.

For me no more the ordinary, nor the mundane
I seek only the miraculous
For my eyes are thus reopened, my ears restored
My heart replenished with the music
Of a thousand sunsets
And all no longer sated
By lesser than perfection.

*

Naked to the world I sit
Free from the clothing of my shame
Vulnerable to all am I.
Devoid of my armour of hatred
Transparent to all that is
I live without my robes of judgement
Yet safe and loving I AM
Without any weapons of anger

Unshielded and unadorned I AM
My truest self exposed
My highest being has no need
Of cover or decor, of perfume or jewels
I Am as true that I AM
I AM as he made me
As it is in the garden

*

One and The Same

I have touched infinity
If only for the briefest
most fleeting of moments.

And while there, as I soared
Across space without moving
As I dove into the sun
Without burning
As I traversed all time
Without aging
I experienced the truth that I AM
The truth of endlessness
The light of boundlessness
The music without beginning or finish.
I have touched the infinite
If only briefly
And here I AM
And here I will remain
For NOW
Chop wood, Carry water.

*

I AM #16

I AM the love of every mother for her children
I AM the joy of children's laughter
I AM the beauty of a field of daisies
Swaying gently in the summer breeze
I AM the abundance of the ocean wave
With all it brings to sandy shore
I AM the silence of snow falling through stars
Of a winter's evening
I AM the peace of birdsong at sunrise
I AM the gratitude of prayer
Over the midday meal
I AM the forgiveness of Jesus
For all his tormentors
I AM the miraculous in the simple
I AM the magnificence in all you perceive mundane
I AM the miracle of being
I AM you

*

A Prayer in Thanks

I AM thankful
I AM grateful to you
My highest self
My silent divine partner
To you I AM giving
My first and highest devotion
I thank you, I love you
I bless you, I trust in you
I cherish you, I treasure you
I worship you, I adore you
I praise you, I honour you, I glorify you
I laud you, I applaud your creation
I celebrate you, I sing your praises
I serve you, I obey you
I submit myself to you

Because of you I AM beautiful
Because of you I AM perfect
I live in constant wonder and awe
And I AM grateful for every moment
Every storm, every raindrop, every tear
Every glint of sunlight, every wisp of cloud
Every breath a whisper of thanks

*

In Spiritus Theos

*

I AM an artist
Occasionally touched by God
Otherwise left
To my own devices
Inspired to a universe
Beyond my understanding
I AM humbled
That what I AM is creator
Created and creation
And with open ears and open heart
Might stumble upon divinity
In my struggles
To remember that touch

*

In the Wake of the Wake RUMInations on a Voyage

In late September of 2012, I was blessed to accompany the late Dr. Wayne Dyer and a few hundred other pilgrims on a Mediterranean cruise organized by Hay House. The theme of this cruise was "In the Wake of Our Ancestors." We ventured all over the eastern Med and saw such incredibly rich spiritual places as Istanbul, Santorini, Ephesus and the house of Mary.

I was tremendously inspired by every stop and by every lecture given by Dr. Dyer. It was the beginning of a new awakening for me. These poems are the first fruits of that awakening. They were all written on the morning that I disembarked from the ship in Civitavecchia, mostly on the bus to the airport in Rome, and completed before my flight landed in Frankfurt, hence the title of this section. There is also the play on words with Rumi who is one of my favourite (and also one of Dr. Dyer's) poets. That is just my bizarre sense of humour at work.

Obviously not all of the lessons of that wonderful journey got all the way through my strong and overactive ego. Nor did many of them stay implanted for long, but it was the beginning of inspiration and of another larger and more profound journey that brings me here to this brief stop on the itinerary.

These poems are the first true confirmation for me of divine channelling. I truly feel that I was merely the vessel through which the spirit expressed itself. I have placed them here, exactly true to form as they first came to me as I journeyed home that day. The titles are what came to me as I was writing.

In Spiritus Theos

*

Civitavecchia
The morning mists whisper softly
Of the new day's potential,
Of glorious adventures,
Of new meanings to old things,
Of love and wonder
Of renewal rebirth and fulfillment,
Of marvels and mysteries
And a world hitherto unexplored.

Their song they sing quietly and gently disappear
As if never here, and we, with sleep filled eyes
Are left to ponder their truth.
Not All.
Poets and dreamers simply smile knowingly.

Highway 1
You missed the sunrise...
Yet still you breathe
Be of good heart my brother
There are countless mornings
In the true firmament
And all days are as morning to the infinite

Pormeriggio
The bean, having been ground
and pressed, soaked and drained
is relegated to the compost to do it all
again, somewhat else.
Latte?

*

*

Fly Away Home
Ah, the wonders of the journey.
From start to finish a unique experience
Incomparable to any other
And still so many impatiently count
The hours since it's departure,
And number even the minutes until it's
Ultimate arrival, not knowing that the route itself
Is rife with meaning.
Thus preoccupied with the affairs of a foreign state,
They sleep to their destination

*

Highway 2
The brush of god
On the canvas of this terrain
Makes an infinite number of impressions
Collecting to be a work available to all
But not seen in main street galleries.

*

Highway3
I AM one with the masterpiece
An insignificant part of the greater fresco
Yet if I am not here
Is it not diminished?

*

Highway 3A
It is harder by far to paint
With the handle of the brush
But even so
The desired work eventually emerges

*

In Spiritus Theos

LIGHT

I knew the words
But they had no meaning
I sang the tune
But had no melody in my song
I said the right things
And made the right motions
With a mind elsewhere concerned.
I walked the right way
But had no direction
I went the right places
But failed to see more than postcards
I knew the right people
And looked the right image
With a heart that was otherwise engaged.
And all too soon
It was over
What now?

*

Sunbeams
In every breath is beauty
In every breath is life
In every twinkling of a star is eternity displayed
In every child's laughter is the universe explained
In the dusty motes of windowed sunlight
Are the joys of God
Dancing, flirting, playfully reminding all
Who will pay attention that such is what we are
Infinite, yet in this form as briefly
As the blink of an eye
Too short a time to spend in anything but joy

*

Grace

I care not what the world may say or do
How can I when you are with me?
And even when you're not
It is I who am absent, adrift
Sailing aimlessly on the small sea
Of my own humours.

What right have I to expect aught of you?
And yet all is mine without my even asking
The sun, the sky, the grounding earth
The soothing waters.
All, and more you give me.
Supply in the garb of abundance
Counsel in the guise of dreams
Remedy in the multitude of flora
Joy in the song and laughter of innocents
Delight in the fragrance of wonder
Refuge from loneliness in your love.

Your gift to me is endless, what more could I desire
As such, what care I, what the world may think?
Those who know you as I do, need say nothing
And those who don't, say what they will
Their clamour like wind in the leaves
Merely a background whisper passing through.
Of little consequence.

*

Poems of Healing

You might find the title to this section strange as few of the poems can be said to have the subject of healing in them. This is for one very simple reason, the healing is not in the poems but was in the writing of them. My healing began with hearing the poems and being compelled to write them down. It was by allowing myself to be open to the process, and grateful for it, that I became a more consciously aware person. By letting these poems come through me I was able to find beauty and inspiration in the world around me once again.

This is the group of poems I most feel emotion over. Not only is it the largest section in this book, it is for me the most powerful. Most of these poems took only minutes to transcribe (as that is my purpose to the true author), but reading and rereading them afterwards, they all strike a strong emotional chord with me.
Even while editing this section I am overcome by reliving the feelings of joy that writing these poems gave to me.

Brett Nelson

*

While you were sleeping
Many things happened
Few that are important
None of them real.
But still it is better that you are awakened
With open eyes you can see
That nightmares are nothing
And slumber but a distraction

*

There is nothing you do not know
There is no music you haven't heard
There is no horizon past what you can see
No undiscovered lands
There is naught but what you've made
Wake up and smell the roses
That you have inspired
Your time has come
Arise with open eyes
Let senses be free
Allow the being
Of all that is you
You are the music
You are the knowledge
You are the dreamer and the dream
You are creation
You are the creator
Be

*

*

Fields of forgiveness
Endless in their immensity
Unlimited in the fragrance
Of their ableness to dissipate
All things that would block
Creation
The coldest souls
The hardest hearts
Are eased and warmed
The tightest fists are opened
A scented wonder, joyful and sweet

Come and lay amongst the blossoms
Allow their scent to heal your heart
A wafted benediction
That eases the soul and dispels the binds
That tie you to vengeance and hatred
For yourself not others
Do you come here
The burden you carry
You gave yourself none other
Be relieved of all you've gathered
The thousand stones you carry
Weightless, frolic and wonder
At the beauty of a life
Not driven by misgiving and distrust
Truly nothing has ever happened
In fields of forgiveness

*

Familiar Friend

I saw your divinity
Peering out from behind your eyes just now
Hi God.
You should let that happen more often
It looks good on you

*

When I think of you my God
Tears of laughter, tears of joy
The sparkling dewdrops of my soul
Come forth to bathe my face
With the radiance of glory
Washing away the layers
Of indifference and illusion
That stand between us
When I know of you my God
The beauty of my inner being
Outpouring though the barriers
Of ego
Emerges to join with you in love
To end the separation, the pain
That once I imagined was real
Not knowing that with you
Alone I could never be
For you are my being
The seed of my soul
The well of my existence
The heaven of my heart

*

*

Without your permission
Life carries on
Despite your strenuous objections
The world still turns
Things are born, others will die
Regardless of your opinion
Without giving one whit
To what you think
The universe unfolds as it should
The sun will rise, the moon will set
The rain will fall, in spite of your tantrums
Your ego, your pouting, your moods, your suffering
Whether you know it or not
Like it or not
Life carries on
And carries you with it

*

Tomorrow is but a promise
And yesterday but a dream
Mere shadows of the
Eternity they represent
Limits of time placed
On that which is limitless
Words fail me
Words pail in comparison
To the truth that is one
Beyond comparison
Beyond my refusal to fathom
The everlasting
The unfathomable endlessness
The abyss of mercy
The infinity of love
That reaches beyond tomorrow
Beyond the promise
Before and after the dream
Never beginning, never ending
One love

*

Brett Nelson

*

To touch the face of God
To feel his breath upon me
To know the presence
On every facet of my being
Bliss eternal

To touch the face of God
To hear her call my name
That the sweetest voice
Would resonate to such as me
Is joy everlasting

To touch the face of God
To feel that touch within me
To see my own face reflected back
And know that it was always thus
Peace

*

In Spiritus Theos

*

Ah summer breeze, from whence do you come
What sultry climes have you crossed
Which exotic ports have you whispered through
On your way to find me
Gentle summer breeze what stories would you tell me
I detect on you the faintest hints of Zanzibar and Bangalore
Have you seen their wonders, can you recant their tales
Fill me with their spiced allure
Oh fickle transient breeze you tease me with your scented passings
You awake my soul with your jasmined caresses
You touch my being with your lavendered tendrils
With perfumed wisps you capture my imagining
Addicting me with longing for more
And yet you go
Ever onward do you wander
Leaving me here to lament
Your oh so brief attendance in my day
So long awaited, so quickly gone
You take no root with me
Ah my meandering friend, where do you go from here
Does the siren of Paris call,
Does Maracaibo await
What news of me do you bring to them
Will you tell them that I sit here waiting, patiently
Expecting the aroma'd gossip of their
Wondrous seductive nights
On your next journey through

*

Brett Nelson

*

When the solidity of this world
Seems to waver and fade
Fear not, All is as it should be

*

In snowbound fog
Is beauty ethereal
Shadowy forms impressed
Upon a white canvas give
Vague suggestions of infinities
Just beyond my conscious.
Possibilities, endless in the mist
Coalesce with time and take the form
Of this passing reality only to become
What I expect and limitedly conform to.
Yet the fog does not dissipate
Nor it's secrets retreat, they only
Sit mystically and await
My eyes true opening

*

In morning
The light of God descends
Warming the earth
Dispelling darkness and shadow alike
Replacing the anxieties of night
With the light of truth, coaxing
Even the most timid to bask
In it's brilliance and glory
Praise be to God

*

27

The greens of spring are deeper
The verdant colours more profound
With eyes newly opened
I see the world as ne'er before
The song of the universe
Sounds richer in my ear
Yet lighter on my heart sits the melody
Harmonies abound in birdsong sweet
And voice angelic with perfect meter
From trickling streams doth rise
To whit the hum of bumbles
Does flit from bloom to bloom
Adding scented bliss to joyous cacophony
Beneath my feet the earth is firmer
Yet softly willing, as if open to suggestion
That even I might add to the grace
To the perfection I experience.
With open heart and open mind
I revel in your abundance my creator
Because of you I sit in wondrous rapture
In the full allowance of knowing
That in you my universe is complete.

*

Be now, but not in haste
Be here, unforced but willing
Allowing and accepted
Repent not..... but the missed
Opportunities to love as God loves
And lo not even this be truly
For in each second of infinity
Lie a thousand tomorrows
Countless nows await your attention
And each chance is reborn
Again and again. For love
As time is one

*

Brett Nelson

*

The echoes of my spirit's calling
Bounce off the walls of my skin
In effort to break free
From this cage of bones

I fling open the doors and windows
Of my soul to feel the eternal
Breeze blow through me, lifting the
Dark shrouds of limit, erasing the
Cobwebs of deceit, reuniting my
True self with it's sacred brethren.

Imprisoned no more, my soul flies
It dissipates in the sea of it's own self
Never diminished, never lessened, ever
Brilliant, radiant and true

Although never truly leaving
It returns to this dusty collection
Of rocks, sea shells and cosmic debris
That for now it calls home
Yet still connected to that which is real
It brings new life to even this

*

Beauty is not in the eye beholding
For tho that eye may shut, beauty remains undiminished
So it is with all things
Should all the clocks be stopped
Eternity flows on unabated
Be the hearts of all the poets stilled
Love grows unaltered
Tho all the ears be closed to hearing
The music of the universe plays on
All of God is, and continues to be
Independent of what is thought
In minds unlit beyond the self

*

In Spiritus Theos

*

I have been home
To that where we all belong
To the miraculous, the magnificent
I have been the Tao that cannot be named
For that is what is
And to touch it is to have it dissolve
To hear it to have it fade away
To see it is to have it disappear
Like morning mist
To describe it is to lose all memory and
Sense of ever being there.
For that is all there is
The being of it
In a place beyond all understanding
Far surpassing physical knowing
More than a feeling
Greater than Heaven
One

*

There is nothing to punish
There is nothing to fear
There is nothing to judge
Because there is nothing here.

In your mind did you make this
In your mind does it live
An illusion of being
Is all it will give.

Be free of this matrix
Relinquish your past
Cut ties to what is
and live from spirit at last.

*

Brett Nelson

To My Ego

Be gone from me O vile pretender!
Brash impostor!
You self proclaimed arbiter of what is.
Your diminutive scope is no longer wanted.
I free myself from you, my true Satan
You who would have me wallow
In the mire of unfulfillment
You hold no sway with who I AM.

No more do I dwell in your
Small acquisitory realm
Mine is the infinite kingdom,
The country without limit
Where such as you cannot be

There is naught for you here
Go elsewhere and peddle
Your cheaply made goods
That serve no purpose but your own

You are not wanted
You are surrendered
I AM so much more without you.

*

In Spiritus Theos

*

Laugh gently
Laugh long
For laughter frees the soul
Laugh loudly
Laugh strong
For laughter flies your heart
Laugh often
Laugh always
For laughter liberates your mind
Laugh freely with an open heart
Laugh joyously and without malice
Laugh openly at your ego and it's foibles
At any and all self imagined faults, remembering
That laughter like love
Is who you truly are

*

Remove your blinders! Your fetters
Your dark glasses, your shades
Open the windows to your soul.
See what you know is there
In your heart of hearts is joy and knowing.

You have seen time and time again
The wonders that await the true believer
Yet still you doubt. Surrender your me-ness
Your three dimensional myopia.

Life lies within and all about you
Endlessness pours forth from your source of all
Dare to be what is written in the halls of the Akashic record.
You are what has always been and what will always be.
You are the music!
You are the light.
What more proof do you need?

*

Brett Nelson

NOT TODAY
What would it be like
To live in an age of glory and wonder?
In an age of miracles and vision?
An age where God is close at hand

What would it be like
To be in a time of brotherhood?
In an era of peace and understanding?
A world where good lies across the land

And what would it be like to
To see beauty unfold around you?
To be part of a world enchanted
A world of love and unity.
'Tis anyone's guess

*

In Spiritus Theos

The Dream is Over

Awake my child and sleep no more
There is no need for slumber
For the night has never been
Never did the sun set
Truly never was there darkness
To cover thee, to cower thee
As was and always will be, only light exists
Shining upon you, lighting your way
Gently dispersing the veil of night
You only thought existed

Arise my child and weep no more
There is no need for mourning
For death has never been
Never did the son set
Truly never was there anything
That could cover thee, or make thee fear
As has ever been only light and life exist
As one shining from you, lighting the way
That others may see, that slumber is no more needed
The dream is over

*

I have seen the truth
A truth so beautiful
It brings tears to my eyes
In memory still, it pales not
And even the most fragrant rose
The sweetest song
The grandest mountain
The softest skin
Are but the most insignificant
Portion, a partial truth in compare
The joy, the love of beauty
How do my eyes see else
What is there after thee?

*

Brett Nelson

*

God's voice is strong and speaks to me
In endless ways I hear it
In sunshine bright, and moonlit night
Through mountain grand, and grain of sand
It gives me strength of spirit.

Though the voices are many, the words are few
The meaning plain and clear
With children's talk and lover's walk
The fall of rain, the flower's gain
All music to my ear.

He tells me that, as it is on earth
So it must be up above
By tree of green, and glen serene
In cry of rook, and babbling brook
God's voice sings "Only Love"

*

Past Perfect?
Bemoaning the doings of yesterday
Keeps us thralled to our history
Reliving victories and failures
Near misses and satisfactions
What would have been, what could have been
What should have been, if only this
If only that...
Ah, the wondrous glories of yesterday
We cling to them and clutch them tight
Applying blame or praise, credit or dishonour
Who should have died, who would have won
All true relevance diminished
With the setting of the sun
And each newly minted yesterday
Just as much over as
the glory that was Rome herself.
Meanwhile today sits idly by, waiting to be lived
Rapidly becoming the yesterday that we will bemoan
Tomorrow

*

Child of Magic

The ever blossoming splendour of God
Is upon the world entire
O sing of joy my prince

His creation a gift to the senses
To be seen by all who are willing
To open their eyes to the truth
O sing of truth joyful son

The very air a fragrance of love
A scent that lingers
On all that open their hearts to it
O sing of love most beautiful child

Its endless song, the music of ecstasy
Sung by every bird and carried to
Every ear that allows its hearing
O sing of music most loving one

The taste of every fruit and flower
The nectar of abundance
Delights the tongue of those
Eager to taste infinity
O sing forever radiant being

The warm and tender touch of earth
A loving caress of the one God
Awaits the every step of those
Who would be worthy
And none more worthy than thou
My perfect one
Scion of love
Child of my imagining
O sing of innocence and beauty
O delight of my soul

*

Brett Nelson

*

In salty tears
Like a summer's rain
I find my god
In the chirrup of crickets
Abetting a moonlit sky
Do I sense her patience
In the babble of children
And the babbling of brooks
I hear the universal melody
Sweet nectar of the life that is
In all things love and laughter
In my newly opened eyes
A chorus a cacophony
Of wonder and joy
She sends me ecstasy
I feel her love
And I well
With salty tears of bliss
Washed in eternal summer rain

*

Your Love

To know love is to know God
To know love is to know peace
To know love is to know joy

Love is serenity
Love is contentment
With you I have found these things
You are the trove of my greatest treasures
You are my greatest wealth
You are my nation, my people, my race
My creed

You are my religion, my patriotism
You are my anthem, you are my hymn
With you I am more than complete
Because of you I am healed
Because of you I am whole
Because of you I am loved
And I am love
You are my love

*

Vision Quest 1

Can you hear the love
In the rustling of the trees
As the gentle breeze
Carries the whisper of God
Gently calling your name

Can you feel the love
On a sunny day
With the sun watching and warming
As a mother who beams radiantly
At her most beloved child

Can you taste the joy
In every raindrop
That falls lovingly from above
Nurturing and nourishing
All that it touches
With the grace of creation

In every note of birdsong
In the thunderous fall of every snowflake
In the soughing of each blade of grass
Is God's endless promise repeated

"Such is the world around you O my child
You are the joy of my creation
Be as I made you, as you were meant to be
This is yours and you are mine
One
Love"

*

In Spiritus Theos

*

Fear nothing
Fear not even death
For death be not proud
It is but the lifting of a veil
That keeps us from seeing
Beauty true and life eternal.

As the seedling discards
The husk from which it's sprung
So too does your ever burgeoning soul
Shed it's dusty cover, this limiting
This stasis, this shell that was only
Ever a holding for that which will not
Be confined.

All is with you
Tho you do not see
The world does not pass away
It waits in life for you to join
Open your eyes to a new day
Allow the breath of God
To dissolve like, so much dust,
The gossamer veil
That blinds and binds you
And leaves you to believe
In a life that is the merest fraction of truth
Reflected by the dimmest of mirrors
Fear nothing. For ever was there naught to harm you
And death does not exist
No matter how much your fears would make it so

*

Brett Nelson

*

There are no secrets to life
Only the truths you keep from yourself
What fault does the universe hold
If you choose not to acknowledge its' wonder
You close your eyes to enlightenment
Yet bemoan the darkness of fear and ignorance
You toil and slave and conjure for death
Though life is myriad around you
You mire and wallow in throes of hatred
While love abounds and cradles you gently
Trapped in the limits of self
In the vain promotion of hubris and ego
You ignore the beauty of all that truly is.

There are no secrets
Only the knowledge that you deny
Buried deep within
'Neath a self imposed bedrock of pain and arrogance
Crying to be heard, the true voice
Light is Life is Love
And all is God
And God is all

*

What a drunken revelry is God's love
Joyful and carefree am I
When imbibed of this spirit
I would dance and frolic
And sing heartily
Giddily do I reel
Unencumbered by the worries
Of ordinary conscious
I would drink deeply of this fine wine
Inhale its' divine bouquet
And live in its influence eternally
Such heady drink this
Such a heavenly vintage
A feast for all the senses
A worthy companion for a world weary soul

Body and Soul

Beneath this collection
Of skin and bone
This assortment of hair and tooth
And all the dust of a thousand stars
Lies the truth
That which this body is
Ever changing, ever dying
Is but a vessel
A shallow cup
A candle holder
Not worthy of the flame
Which gives it purpose
The immortal, the infinite
That which cannot, nay will not
Be restrained directs this
Jumble of notes, paying it no heed
For none is needed
And when finished with this
Pile of cosmic rock and dirt
Allows it to become
That which it came from
For all that is not spirit
Begins and ends as it must
As ash and dust

*

Brett Nelson

Words to a Young Man

Be patient my child
Your life has yet to begin
You are but an embryo
In the womb of creation
And all that has happened to you
Are the stirrings of a soul
Waiting to be born

You are a chrysalis
Striving to emerge
From this illusionary shelter
From this confinement of form
Soon your wings you'll spread
And lofted will you be
Defying all the laws
Of your own making
On your journey to the infinite

But wait my child
Be patient
Divine time knows not your deadlines
It awaits only your perfection
Which you have yet to see
A moment longer
By the hours of God
And life begins truly

*

Love is as God
Patient and unrushed
Like a blade of grass through concrete
Or a river deep in the canyon
Etched by eons of wear
Relentless and unstoppable
Gentle and unending
Changing all within its' path
Its' one goal irresistible
Life

*

In Spiritus Theos

*

Put not your faith in the works of man
Old as pyramids be
They crumble to dust
All the most grandiose plans
But temporary mementoes to hubris

Put not your faith in the works of man
Glass and steel
Concrete and stone
Mere elements, broken down
By scant tickings of this earthly clock

Put not your faith in the works of men
Empires and traditions fall by the wayside
Withered like leaves from a tree
Long dead, its' fall not heard
By any living now

Put not your faith in the works of men
The greatest poems
The grandest songs
Naught but whispers
Scattered by ancient winds
Themselves faint echoes of
A grandeur passed

Nay, put not your faith in the works of man
Temporary and fleeting as they may be
But in the works of God
For mountains have little memory of pyramids
Rivers tell no tales of empire
And even these, ageless by our standard
Will pass before the mighty eye of heaven
To disappear with little comment
From our eternal creator

*

Brett Nelson

The Pinnacle

I awake this morning
To the realization that
Everything up to this point
Is naught but illusion
All the yesterdays
The torments, the struggles
My histories, my past
Have all been my resistance
To the eventuality of truth.

There is only here
There is only now
There is only I
Not the me of this flesh
Nor this supposed solidity of bone
With its' risings and fallings,
Its' slumbers, comas and
Dubious conscious states.

No. There is only I
The I of eternity
The I of the storm
The light of all souls
The life of all things
And my part but a fragment
A single raindrop in a monsoon of possibility
My separation only a figment
A thread in an endless fabric
Never beginning, Never ending
Infinite and eternal
What a glorious day this will be

*